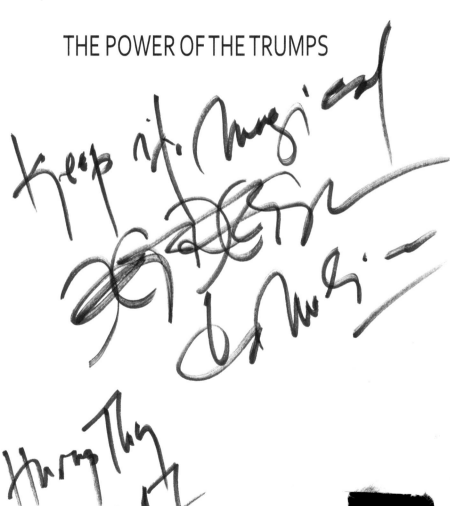

# THE POWER OF THE TRUMPS

# THE POWER OF THE TRUMPS

## a subtle burst

**CAMELIA ELIAS**

EYECORNER PRESS

*THE POWER OF THE TRUMPS:*
*A SUBTLE BURST*

Published by EYECORNER PRESS
in the series **Divination Books**

April 2017, Thy, Denmark

ISBN: 978-87-92633-38-5

Cover design, image, and layout: Camelia Elias

Images of the Tarot:

**Marseille Tarot by Jean Noblet,** 1650
reconstructed by Jean-Claude Flornoy.

With kind permission by Roxanne Flornoy.

Printed in the UK and US

*FOR FRIGG*

# Contents

# Stumbling into a Subtle Burst

The text in front of you is based on a series of video lectures, where I talk about the power of the trumps. What you read here is basically the transcript of those lectures. I like the idea of words following voice, as this, in a way, is something I cover right here.

I read sequences of three cards, just the trumps of the Marseille Tarot, with a have a specific aim in mind.

I intend to teach something about the power of the Tarot trumps, both at the individual and collective level.

That is to say, I look at the cards as they appear next to one other, but at the same time I describe their force individually.

What interests me is power that's not so in your face, and there-fore often stronger. This won't come as a surprise to occultists and animists, spiritual workers and other good folk who help people with their internal mess.

For this group, power that manifests subtly is power that's inter-esting, power that's raw, dangerous, and not safe.

While this little book is another way of saying that you can learn what to do with the Tarot trumps in terms of thinking of them as representations of embodiment, function, and voice, it also gives you insight that runs at a subtler level, where what I explore is precisely this:

A burst of power that's unmediated by culture.

This is a tall order, as it's impossible to escape the symbolic mind-set we all grow up with, and by 'symbolic mindset' I don't mean to suggest things like equating cups with love, but rather the mindset that tells you you're a success if you earn a lot of money, have a good education, an honest wife, and obedient children.

Now, doesn't all that make you soft in your knees? Of course it does, especially if you happen to be in the middle of the altar, saying yes, and buying the promise of everlasting happiness.

Such is the work of belief: It's all symbolic, and we know it. It's all delusion, and we like it.

But here's what I do in this series, other than laugh at our beliefs. I employ a simple method:

I say something obvious. Then I ask you to think about it in different ways, and then I encourage you stop thinking according to received perceptions.

§

Many talk about how the Tarot speaks to them. Indeed there is such a thing. Voice is the most magical tool we have, and it looks like inanimate objects also have it.

But how concrete is what we hear? Putting what we hear into words so that our understanding is going somewhere is also an act of magic.

What I do in this book that I haven't done in my other divination books, or my other numerous writings in the social media, is stress the bursting quality of the trumps when it is experienced at the subtle level.

By 'subtle' I mean the level that's in between worlds, on the horizon line where the seen and the unseen mingle in an oracular way, which is to say, the poetic way, the way that bursts open our perceptions.

This is less mysterious than it sounds.

Just ask yourself: How many times have you sat with the images of the Tarot and had the feeling that although you see what you see, you also see more? I bet your answer to this is, 'many.'

Why do you think that is?

Because subtlety has a voice. And this voice is more articulate than you think. It has a wider range than your whisper: 'Here be Dragons. I'm reading the Tarot and it feels like riding the hedge.'

So you start noticing the unseen that stares you in the face. The obvious is mysterious. It's mysterious because it's sharp and has the face of the two worlds shape-shifting.

You get a question about relationships and off you go with reading embodiments, color, form, function, and fancy.

How weird is that?

It's weird because you take this job seriously, because you trust your feet firmly planted in two worlds. You're not riding this hedge because you want to act on dictations, cultural images and what's appropriate in their constructions. You're into other creations.

But what do you see? What **can** you see? Are you reading the Tarot with your full body, or are you transmitting consecrated thoughts, good ones, but sometimes uninspired because they are not yours? Where do you go, when you want to see what's what for yourself?

'I need to get there fast,' the Fool says. 'No time for walks here. I'll get in my car and teleport myself . . . Oops, it looks like I bumped into something. What was that?'

Getting there fast, wherever it is you need to go to, is a great intention. But what if you forget something essential? Namely, that all Tarot readings are subject to conditions that change?

What you point to right now, when you look at a simple-three card draw, can be contradicted by a fourth card.

You may think: 'Well, I was too eager. I brought this accident on myself.'

But wait. Stop and look. What else is the Fool saying?

'Who's that other person falling out of the Tower?'

'What if it wasn't my fault?'

This is what happens when someone tricks you into taking the car, when you'd be better off walking, and to take him along as a clandestine passenger.

Someone who tells you: 'All this slow motion, you can do better. I'll give you directions.'

Boom, the car hits a rock, or more rocks, the ones the Magician throws into the air that he pretends are his magic tools on his table, and before you know it, you're in for a ride, all right, but one that renders you in the ditch.

So all is well until it's not anymore.

You sigh. At least you can blame this on someone else. You can blame it on the fourth card, the conman.

§

If you ever get such card combinations that go from featuring single people on them, to ones that feature several people on them, do you ever ask:

Who are these others? Do I know them? How do they impact on me? By way of force or inspiration?

See, one of the guiding questions in all of my readings is in fact this very question:

Who is doing what to whom?

In my examples here, I offer a concrete meditation on the problem of agency. I ask you to think about the power to act and who holds it. Is this power in the picture at all?

The Tarot trumps are very clever at prompting us with this observation, and how we go from noticing who and what we're dealing with to the more refined, 'yes, but how does this impact on me, or the situation I'm in?'

We have people cards, we have nature cards, and we have cards that tell us, 'you're also going to die'.

Well, thank you cards.

It's good to know when a storm is coming, so I can call that a natural catastrophe if I see Judgment and the Tower together.

One big cloud, and before you know it, everyone is directly affected. I don't need to speculate: 'Who did this to me? Who are the others?'

The other question that interests me in this series of looking at the subtle and bursting power of the trumps is the question of timing.

Not so much timing in the sense of observing the dynamics between fast cards and slow cards – we've just had an example of that here, the Fool is slow, the Charioteer is fast – but more in the sense of when the time is right for something.

When you come to the cards with your question, you do so because the time is right for you to get answers that are more aligned with what your reality is and how it confronts you head on.

After all, the only reason why you read cards is because you want to get away from culture and its discontents.

You may know, culturally speaking, that it's a good idea to finish that education, stop bumming around and get in the fast lane.

But what if the time is right for something else? What if you're done with working for an institution, and the time is right to walk away, do something else?

You don't quite know what that is, because you're not trained to think outside of what culture dictates, but you know what you don't know that you **do know.**

We call this logical intuition.

So how do you see it in the cards when the time is right for something?

This question is what I like to think of as the subtle burst in our readings, as it makes us go beyond symbolic power, beyond familiar patterns of thinking.

When the Tarot speaks to you, it doesn't speak in a language that's borrowed. It speaks in a language that you understand as you cross the line of what's appropriate.

Come, ride on this hedge, and learn to think what not to think, learn to read the like the devil, and get that penetrating vision going by reading the damn cards.

LE FOV

# I Don't Know

'Why regret?' people often ask me, whenever I read the card of the Hanged Man. Well, you see, traditionally, and by tradition I mean the evidence we find in old texts about the use of cards, the Hanged Man has been associated with treason.

You betray your country, you'll find yourself hanged, and then drawn and quartered in the city square.

This is a most gruesome practice of punishment, when the traitor would be tied to a wooden frame and then stretched beyond what the body's own flexibility would allow for. Sometimes being quartered simply meant being chopped up with an axe.

This public act had one message only: 'It's regretful that some can't be loyal. The law punishes treason.'

As people would be witnessing the final breath of the tortured man or woman, they'd have their own regrets, secret and unspoken of. This is a response appropriate for what culture wants:

To instill fear.

Culture doesn't like unusual, revolutionary ideas, because such ideas give you a taste for freedom. Freedom is culturally inappropriate because it can't be regulated, constricted or contained. Freedom is bad news for culture, and culture punishes bad news.

Most modern Tarot readers would go: 'You see things differently,' in their reading of the Hanged Man, and they'd be correct in their assumption.

But.

What most fail to tell you is that seeing things differently can get you hanged, drawn and quartered, regretting your own actions, and ultimately having an ecstatic experience that you can't share with anyone because it's most certainly followed by death.

Let us not forget that the trump following The Hanged Man is, after all, Death.

But think of this situation:

So you say to yourself:

'I'm so going to make the right choice here. The blondie is the one for me. I like the wisdom of the brunette, she's older and more mature, but the blondie is better for my image.'

This is the Charioteer speaking, having the confidence of the young man, who, after some considerable vacillation and hesitation, is finally making his choice.

Whatever internal conflict there may still be inside the heart, will be swept under the polished shining armor.

What's an image good for, if you don't fling it to the public, flash it in all its virile construction? But what if you betray something in your choice? What if the blonde woman is not the right one for you?

What if your heart is somewhere else, in fact gone in the opposite direction, taking the path you didn't choose?

Ay, here comes the Hanged Man situation. Regret. The grand standstill. Now what?

Sometimes you bring this on yourself. Sometimes you're simply subject to external conditions.

Sometimes you think you have just enough power to control your choices, but, as the image of the Lovers suggests, this is yet another grand illusion.

What do you suppose the presence of Cupid is there for? To inflame your passion, your love? Get real.

Cupid is in the picture as a subtle, yet nasty reminder of the fact that you are never in control.

You are always at the mercy of chance.

If you're into prayers, then pray to Cupid that he shoots his arrow in such a way so that you experience the outcome as one of alignment:

Your heart in alignment with your conditions.

§

I don't get this common Tarot talk: 'Follow your heart', pertaining to the 'meaning' of the Lovers card.

Yeah, right. Thank you very much. Can I now, please, also know what my heart wants?

See, there's a reason why we talk about Mystery Traditions, most of them lost to the many.

These initiatory methods of integrating your unconscious fears and desires with your conscious mind had a very good function: The function of saving you the trouble of regretting your choices, of imagining a number of 'what if' situations.

'What if I had picked the other one, the other man or woman, job, house, lover, and so on?'

If you think you have time to speculate, then by all means.

Suppose you realize all this while you're hanging.

Suppose you realize that the little agency you have in the Lovers card, the flashing illusion of agency in the Charioteer's card is now completely gone, and you have one option only:

To listen to the clock: tick, tock, tick, tock.

Suppose you're aware of the fact that there's a lot in between the tick and the tock of the clock.

You become aware of the impressions that come to you, the tick, the tock, and other ones in between.

Will someone save you, cut your rope, or not? Does it even matter? You're listening to the clock. That's where you're at.

Whoa, that's pretty close to the mysterious, ecstatic experience.

Suddenly the urge to 'keep going' has a deeper resonance for the Hanged Man, than the one we associate with the Charioteer and his horses, or the Lover and his dames.

§                                          ·

Here's what I say:

**Don't just think:**
'I can follow my heart,' when you have no idea about what your heart wants.

**Don't just think:**
'I can control these horses,' when you have no idea about the nature of horses, or what comes next. What if a storm comes and topples your carriage? How confident will you be with your head in the ditch?

**Don't just think:**
'I'm having a new perspective,' when you're hanged. Who did this to you anyway? You don't even know.

Unless you're Odin or a skilled yogi who knows exactly what he's doing and why, you have no chance of surviving just because you have a different perspective, because you know things.

§

Put more succinctly, what is missing here is a clear sense of agency. Agency is presumed through will power, but is not really in the close-up picture.

The Lover thinks he has it, though it's Cupid who has it. The Charioteer is convinced he has it, though the horses may have a different opinion. The Hanged Man hopes he has a whole lot of it, because, once transcended, he will be like God.

But to what extent are the Lovers, the Charioteer, and the Hanged Man aware of what they (must) give up in order for agency to occur?

If we look closely, we see that here are three trumps in the Tarot pack whose power is actually all about teaching you the value of 'NOT KNOWING'.

§

Try this instead:

'**I don't know** which one to pick. I accept whatever fate has in store for me. Chance is entertaining, and I can relax. It's not like any of it has any meaning.'

'**I don't know** where I'm going. The horses pull this thing, but I haven't a clue as to whether this image of the winner is going the same place as the horses.'

'**I don't know** what I'm seeing. I don't even know what to regret. In the final analysis, I don't know how much longer I can last.'

§

Start with '**I don't know,**' and see how far your choice, confidence, and new perspective will take you.

A long way, I hope. It's in this humility that we find the power of contemplative action.

REFERENCES:

For an overview of the meaning of the Tarot trumps à la ancient texts, consult the following reference book:

*Explaining the Tarot: Two Italian Renaissance Essays on the Meaning of the Tarot Pack,* edited, translated and commented by Ross Sinclair Caldwell, Thierry Depaulis, Marco Ponzi. Oxford: Maproom Publications, 2010.

# Your Luck is Made

'Look, the Wheel of Fortune. That means luck, right?'

'Wrong'.

That's what you tell the eager ones. What you call being lucky is subject to conditions that change. What you call being unlucky is subject to conditions that change.

So what's happening here?

Three creatures are caught in a wheel, and they spin so fast that you can't even see their faces anymore. Is that lucky? Is that unlucky? We don't know.

BUT WE KNOW THIS:

1) if you go too fast, or for too long under conditions that dehumanize you, it's not good.
2) if you identify too much with what you're being caught into, it's not good.
3) if you have no sense of distinct power because you're at it with everyone else, it's not good.

If you think that the previous talk about lack of agency is scary, think of this one. Here no one has agency. We don't know who turns the damn wheel? Who is behind it?

Can you ever catapult yourself off that drudgery, and become an individual again? What would it take to get your power back?

'My girlfriend wants to get married and have children right away,' a concerned young man tells you. He wants to know what married life will be like.

'It will be like hell,' I tell him, while pointing to the Wheel of Fortune.

'But, but that's a sign of being fortunate, is it not?', he insists, while also pointing to the Emperor:

'I can decide how things will go.'

'Well, you can do that,' I say to him, 'you have the power to de-termine when you've had enough of the routines that dehuman-ize you, but once caught here, in this wheel, your luck is not made if your self-empowering act ends in madness.'

I point to the Moon following the Emperor following the Wheel of Fortune.

'Marriage is not for everyone,' I say, 'and children even less, though most people would disagree. So, for you, it's hell.'

The Emperor's eyes go blank. He fancies the marriage, but the children part scares the shit out of him.

A clear picture.

§

HERE'S WHAT I SAY:

What's the use of imperial power if it ends in shadow, moonlight reflecting projections, and general misunderstandings?

Everyone is howling and no one gets a thing. That's not your clas-sical recipe for great fortune.

If you get caught in what you resist already, it's not enough to say that you can decide on changing the plan.

If you end up carrying too much of the initial drudgery into the new plan, you can be sure that you'll reach a state where you won't even recognize yourself anymore. Who is this dog?

The Wheel of Fortune maintains some human shape. The Moon has none of that. The Moon card is the first in the sequence of trumps that features no humans in it. Why is that?

What do we need to forget? Or remember? The city is still in the picture, so you're not quite in the wild yet. Who would even survive in the wild? Surely not the hopeless romantic.

§

Think of it in these terms:

If marriage is on the table, the Wheel of Fortune is not a sign of fortune.

If relationship is on the table, the Emperor is not a sign of sharing. If family is on the table, the Moon is not a sign of harmony.

What of agency again?

If you think the cards in the previous talk show problems where agency and will-power is concerned, even as we may talk about self-sacrifice, then think about the Wheel of Fortune.

A nasty card where the individual is concerned.

So we're back to the notion of chance. Who knows who turns the Wheel?

If it's the Hanged Man, then you can wait a while. Expect nothing.

If the Lovers turn your wheel, say a prayer to Cupid. You really need that luck.

If the Charioteer, expect the fifth wheel to your wagon to cause some problems.

If the Emperor, sigh with relief. What a break. Now something will happen.

That is to say, if the Emperor can avoid going nostalgic on you, imagining too many things, or being a little afraid. Some Emperors prefer to rule over a kingdom that has no children in it, or women, or old people.

**Don't think** fortune is made in spinning gold.
**Don't think** power is sovereign when divided.
**Don't think** fear or fascination is reality.

Your luck is made when you sit quietly, at night, and know that kings also lose their heads when the wheel turns.

§

The thing to remember is that some cards carry the idea of agency, the power to act, while others suggest no such thing.

To assign fortune to the Wheel of Fortune would mean to assign power to it. The Wheel of Fortune has power by virtue of the power of impermanence, but impermanence is not subject to human agency and intervention.

Although we may say, 'cut,' 'new rule, or 'stop that wheel', we would only be able to act in this way if the means to free others, or make offerings, were available to us.

If imperial power is subject to distorted, diluted, and deluded conditions, then it acquires no more agency than the saying, 'what goes around, comes around,' which is based on observation not action.

Sometimes you have power, **but** get nowhere. Sometimes you don't have power, **and yet** you get things done.

And there's nothing new under the sun.

# Busted Light

If there's nothing new under the sun, a lot of things happen in the moonlight. This is because the moon craves the light of the sun.

Astronomically speaking, as the moon chases after the sun, it's little wonder where we got the symbolic idea of associating the Moon with desire. The moon is a problem card because it's a natural significator for our fears and desires.

The anxiety felt in the common question, 'What if I'm not good enough?' discloses both the desire to be more, and the fear of being less.

But what is more and what is less? What is 'more' relative to? What is 'less' relative to?

Here comes the Sun to illuminate your speculations.

It's simple: In questions of adequacy, you only have the others to rely on. Their constitutive gazes upon you will tell you: 'Yes, you're awesome', or 'No, you can work harder on your image.'

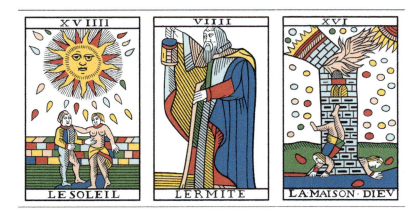

But whose truth would this be? Yours or theirs? Why do we need others to have our sense of being in the world validated? And what world are we talking about?

To give myself as an example:

It would be pointless to go to the academic illuminati and expect validation for my fortunetelling skills. If they'd grant me that, they'd call it something else.

We call this vocabulary and being skilled at finding names for whatever disturbs us, or enchants us, for that matter.

Likewise, it would be pointless to bring my talk of semiotics, the reading of signs, or semantics, the knowledge of how we create meaning, to the cartomantic community, even though that's exactly what I do when I read cards: I activate my semiotic and semantic vocabulary. Not to mention my linguistic and grammatical competence.

The point is that when we seek validation, when we seek other people's radiance and brilliant gazes of approval on us, we must remember what tower we're in, before we get either too enthusiastic or too depressed.

WHEN THAT IS SAID, THINK:

What good does it do the Hermit to illuminate what the Sun already does quite as a matter of course, and much more brilliantly?

To doubt what you share, the warmth and light of others, only has the function of bringing down whatever tower you're in.

Over-speculation, personal crisis and weariness, run counter to the idea of an intimate relationship, of love.

The Sun is a card of love, not the Lovers. The Hermit kills it. How can you contain all that light in your little lamp? Why would you even want to do that?

There's a time for the Hermit, as there's a time for the Sun, but not in that order, first the Sun and then the Hermit.

§

'My relationship is busted,' a philosopher tells me.

'Yeah,' I say. 'Do you know why?', I ask, while looking at the Tower and just knowing.

'Well, you know,' he says, 'she accused me of not trusting her.'

'That sounds about right to me,' I say, while looking at the Tower.

'Yeah,' the philosopher, retorts, imitating my tone, and adding irritation to it:

'How would you know what's between us?'

'I don't know,' I say. 'I'm just looking at the Tower.'

'You wanted illuminations that you could control. On and off goes the lamp. But when the power of the Sun gets channeled through your little lamp, expect an explosion.'

So it goes.

The philosopher is still thinking about it.

§

If you don't have enough energy for the grand love, or, if you only have energy for your own contemplative inclinations, then stay away from love that requires sharing, mutual respect, and great warmth and light.

The Hermit has no business stepping into the Sun, when all he wants, by virtue of his age or wisdom, is a dark cave.

Here comes the Tower. But the Tower is no cave. A busted tower hit by lightening will affect everyone present in it.

If you have an inclination for solitude, then make sure you don't seek partnership or friendship. You will only contribute to bringing the house down.

Doubting the sun has rarely brought anything good with it. At best, seek shelter from it, if you find it too hot, too assuming, full of brilliance and devotion. Here comes the Sun, rising every morning, unfailingly, whether we see it or not. 'How irritating', some may think.

Bottling up pressure from too much doubt and speculation is bound to find release in something that will turn into forced validation.

§

THE LESSON HERE IS THIS:

The ones who behold the Sun don't need to resort to sudden bursts that validate their image.

The ones who behold solitude don't need others to tell them what to think.

The ones who behold ruin, don't need an optimism that's not theirs.

Whether cards of relationships, warm or ruined, whether cards of solitude, imposed or self-imposed, cards tell us that we're alone.

Repeat after me: **I'm always alone.**

When you fall from that Tower, you're alone. There may be others down with you, but you're still alone.

Under the sun with another you're still alone.

Cards tell stories of positioning.

'You are here now', they say.

And so you are, if you care to look, to accept what stares you in the face: light or lightning.

# Sometimes You Cry

You do all the right things, you're fair and judicious, you can let go. And still you cry.

I can't remember what cards we read in my cartomancy class, but I found myself saying something essential to one of the students who expressed slight anxiety towards my Zen attitude to all things, manifested as standing clear of emotion, avoiding over-thinking, and just breathing.

Easier said than done, as this attitude requires a lot of trust and trust is not something we grow up with.

The student wanted to know about my thoughts on crying and if I ever did it.

I said this to her:

It's not a question about not crying because that's stupid, or ir-relevant. Bodily sensations turn into emotions.

That's a fact.

The point is to be there, present, when this happens, and know exactly what your body does, which is respond, not take on a 'meaning' ride.

The art is to know that this response has no meaning whatsoever. If you know that, then you stand clear of actions derived from emotion that you may be seduced into assigning meaning to.

'Well,' I thought to myself after that tirade: 'That's pretty commonsensical. Sometimes we cry. And that's all there is to it.'

§

Now, the astonishing thing is not what you hear nowadays as part of the mainstream mindfulness program that dictates: 'Give yourself permission to cry'.

What's astonishing is that when you sometimes cry, you do so as part of your default nature, not as part of any program dictating anything, even when this program is deemed superior to other programs.

I'm thoroughly amused when I hear it all the time: 'Give yourself permission to cry.' 'Give yourself permission to do this and that.' 'Give yourself permission to love yourself.' 'Give yourself permission to not feel shame. There's nothing to be ashamed of.'

One grows ever so tired of all these permissions. One grows ever so tired of all self-empowering speech. Why can't we accept the fact that when sometimes we cry, we do so because that's all there is to it? Why can't people get it that this line, 'because that's all there is to it,' is enough.

Giving permission, even if that be myself embodying the ultimate self-empowering agency, 'I, and I mean, **I** [double stress here] give myself permission . . . ' smacks too much of culture, the culture that now dictates:

'Be good to yourself, love yourself, don't give any fucks, refute all critique, you're perfect.'

This is all good and sound advice, if only all this self-love and perfection would not be so goddamn intangible.

As in the case with our example of knowing what the heart wants in order to follow it commonsensically, we also want to ask here:

What is the premise for the self-love, for the perfection of self? It's not like we exist in a vacuum. We exist in the eyes of the beholder.

§

Someone comes to me, looks at her cards, and starts crying.

Sobbing she says:

'I do all the right things, I'm fair and judicious, and I can let go. And yet, the woman with the sword makes me cry'.

If I were to express an opinion, I'd say I can only agree that any woman with a sword in her hand should make us cry, but I'm here to do more than express an opinion.

I'm here to point to three cards, full of woman power, and how we can understand the process of going for it and getting it, formalizing it, and then changing lanes.

What happens to your royal consecrations, your degrees and professional confidence, when the truth is that sometimes you cry, you spill your waters, and hope to God that your naked body can behold all that star power coming down on you, while you're out in the woods, away from the city and its masks and costumes?

You see, it's when we see these good cards on the table, each embodying very different functions, that we understand the meaning of the phrase, 'and that's all there is to it'.

What does giving yourself permission for anything have to do with anything?

JUST THINK:

Sometimes, when you're done with your duties, you go home and take a bath, and that's all there is to it.

Why does this need no further explanation? Conversly, why does, 'sometimes we cry' need explanation? Why do we need to sentence ourselves to the latest phrase in vogue? Why bring in injunctions that we pass on ourselves even when they are inappropriate?

'Give yourself permission to feel bad. That's a good girl.'

We're only in the courthouse if we see ourselves needing a courthouse. But are courthouses home? They are not. They are cold and impartial. They are not exactly a place for pleasure: 'Give yourself permission to drink more wine, before you sign here.'

§

In a more radical context, what if the truth is that there is never any need for anything?

**Don't think,** 'here comes the Empress, the nurturing and clever woman.' What if she's just clever, or just nurturing sitting on shit you don't even want to come close to?

**Don't think,** 'here comes Justice, the woman of method, she's going to win my case.' What if she's the Devil's advocate in a nurturer's costume or no costume, holding only a promise for deliverance?

**Don't think,** 'here comes the Star, all my sins can be washed away. I can give myself permission to sin some more.'

Sometimes you cry.

§

Sometimes your crying is completely independent of your permissions, and feelings that you have and feelings that you think you should have.

Now you're welcome to ask: Is there a difference?

No, there isn't. Your feelings are just thoughts in your head. Your feelings are language. The language that the Empress speaks, that Justice formalizes, and that the Star sings.

Your language is never yours. Your thoughts are never yours. Your feelings are never yours.

Sometimes all the good cards that have a good message for you can still make you cry, and that's all there is to it.

# What's in a Name?

What is a teacher good for, if she can't participate in resolving conflict?

In my 20 years of teaching experience this question almost became a mantra. But addressing conflict is not always free of conflict. The reason for this is because we live though perceptions.

You may think you're doing all the right things, you may think you possess fairness, and are capable of generosity – as seen in the previous example when the Empress, Justice, and the Star got together – and yet you may find that what you do is also perceived as dominance, discipline, and overbearing.

Who is right and who is wrong?

This question is big enough to create conflict and tension in the body.

Tension in the body manifests as illness and a sense of heaviness. On the intangible and unconscious level, as you feel your heart as hard you start wondering how to make it soft again.

In spiritual contexts such as Buddhism, softening the heart is a primary aim. A soft heart gives you access to equanimity and flow.

But what does having a soft heart mean? What does being in the flow mean?

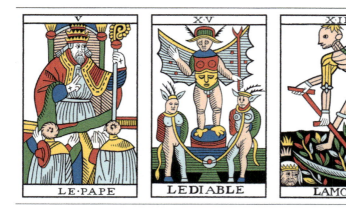

If you have a spiritual adviser or mentor you consult, you may hear this message:

'You channel a lot of demons. Cut it out.'

If you have a family doctor or a psychologist you consult, you may hear this message:

'You're addicted. You give in to obsession. Cut it out.'

Often this advice comes in response to the question on the table about how to solve conflict. Fair enough. But when the conflict is inner, felt at the heart level, then this question, while on the ta-ble, remains either inarticulate, or difficult to formulate.

Why is this so?

Because of what we call the unconscious.

The best way I can think of explaining the unconscious is to point to how the process of acquiring a sense of self occurs. This is a big area, and each discipline, from psychoanalysis to neuroscience, has different things to say about it.

THINK OF IT IN THIS WAY:

After several attempts at recognizing what you are – when you realize already at infant level that you're not exactly your mother, the one you mirror yourself into – something obvious hits you:

**You are your name.** Not only that, but you realize also that if you don't like this name, you can just change it.

The latter is considered a form of adolescent rebellion, and it's interesting to observe, but the process of 'selving' is the same, boiling down to this realization:

You are your name.

You're conscious of what that means because you're always in the process of branding your name, selling it, transacting with it, negotiating with it and for it.

You may finish an education, but it's not you who gets the degree and a diploma. It's your name. You take this name and plaster it all over job applications, and eventually you get to pop the champagne. But what gets celebrated is your name, not you.

So far so good. You're now conscious of **what** you are, not **who** you are.

But then something else happens.

Freud would say, welcome to your death drive. Your instincts rule. You're way more than your conscious name.

Lacan, Freud's main interpreter would say, your unconscious is language, a borrowed thing. You are a 'thing' of chance.

Neuroscientists such as Candace Pert would say, your unconscious is your body.

Medical doctors would say, your unconscious sits in your gut. The gut has an intelligence that the conscious mind does not.

§

We can't escape the simple fact that the body beholds our brain and the mind. But consciousness itself seems to be outside of the body.

Ooo, here we enter the woo woo territory.

You start obsessing already: Who is this 'I' beyond the name? See, that's a very good question. One of the Devil's favorites, because it creates conflict.

Time to bring in the exorcists.

If you're brave enough, or had the good fortune to come across a teacher who enlightens you on the spot: 'Relax, soften your heart, nothing has substance, you're nothing', then you can say hello to Death and stop channeling the demons of your existential crisis.

When we think of the Popes of the world as spiritual teachers, exorcists, counselors, or medical doctors, what we think of is a name:

'This one can fix it,' we think, as we spill our guts while the clock is ticking. Tick, tock, tick, tock. 'Isn't he done with that blessing yet? All that patronizing?'

But you keep going. You fill the good doc with your obsessions, if you can even articulate them, and then you hear the verdict:

'Nothing can save you but death. Either you cut the crap, or you wait until you die.'

The good news is that nothing lasts forever. The bad news is the nothing lasts forever. This is a good meme that circulates in public consciousness.

Enjoying your symptoms, clinging to emotion or intellect, will only get you so far. Manipulating others into believing your stories, or your change of names, will only make them say: 'Off with your head. We're so done with this'.

THE LESSON TO PONDER HERE IS THIS:

**Don't think** that only the competent ones with a name and reputation can solve a conflict.

They can, but it would require intense listening on your part. If you happen to channel demons, then your focus will be elsewhere, on your addiction, aversion, compulsion, worry, envy, jealousy, and so on.

**Don't think** that your inner demons are cool, simply because you heard someone say that the Devil represents passion, attraction, and cunningness.

It can, but in a way that demonstrates restlessness and a disconnect between the body and regular peace of mind. Your unconscious is the Devil you don't know.

**Don't think** that putting an end to your clinging is a tragedy.

It hurts to remember that 'remembering your name' means exactly nothing, but it's worth remembering it nonetheless.

§

When the student is ready, the teacher will appear, the Indian saying goes, that some attribute to the Buddha.

CONSIDER THIS:

You are ready when your heart is soft.

You're ready when the Devil you know is **not** unconsciously the Devil you actually don't know but serve, one way or another.

Just listen.

When the Pope's finger goes up, it's not always as a blessing. It's a gesture that can point to many things.

It can point to you and your unconscious demons, not just your name given in baptism, your name Death will help you inscribe on a tombstone.

As dead, you're of little use to the living. Keep alive, and ask for your name that only your gut knows, your unconscious knows, and your body knows.

What 'you' know is nothing.

The only thing you can know with some degree of certainty is that you're here now, breathing, reading these words.

But the Devil will convince you that you know everything already. And if you 'feel' that you don't know it, he will promise to give it to you.

Ay, the pacts many have made in exchange for knowledge . . .

We all know how those stories ended:

With the big essentializer, Death, laughing at you, as you're clinging to your name, the one you 'know' you have, because the Devil himself gave it to you, in baptism.

§

REFERENCES:

For a heavily Freudian influenced Tarot interpretation, see Alejandro Jodorowsky's, *The Way of the Tarot* (2009). Destiny Books.

For inspiration on how the body acts as your unknown territory, see Candace Pert's, *Your Body Is Your Subconscious Mind* (2004). Sounds True Publishing.

# The Art of Resilience

If you go from 1 to 21, disregarding the other steps even if they don't come in their ordinary numerical order, you may discover that in the process that you've just managed to lose your breath.

Having the skills to do something is one thing. Having the skills to survive while you're at it is another thing.

Magic work, which the interpretative art always is, begins with a moment of enchantment. First, you look over your shoulder to make sure no one is after you. Next, you in-spirit yourself. You conjure forces with your mind, and then off you go to tell a story.

You can say to yourself: 'Now I will enchant the world.'

You can take the necessary steps of preparation, and then test what there is to test:

Is there an interest in this thing? Am I giving others what they what to hear, or serve because I'm the best at it and can't help it?

There's always a public out there. In fact, without the others we would never get a sense of what home means, or what being familiar with something means.

But it doesn't follow that just because you're familiar with something, you're also familiar with what the public wants.

It may well be the public wants a package solution, the key to all the problems in the world, but when we talk about raised consciousness, what we talk about is not second-guessing what kind of judgments go into holistic approaches.

The Magician may be well versed in selling his tricks to the public, but without maintaining a resilient mind, a mind that focuses by de-concentrating, he will never be able to get past a mere promise.

§

As a writer, I get lots of writing-related correspondence, some campaigns inviting me to join this or that writing class. I always consider taking a new class, even though teaching creative writing is something I've done myself. I like to learn new things.

But I can tell you this: I never embark on a course that describes its implicit premise in this way:

> Hey there Camelia,
> So. You've had struggles. Big ones.
> Debt. Addiction. Raised by mean chimpanzees who didn't share their bananas with you. But you overcame those obstacles, found self-love, and now you're living the life of your dreams!
>                                            – Marie Forleo selling *The Copy Cure*

Now, I get this enchantment. I get that this is an invitation to consider just how easy it is to find a topic to write about, and sell, as it's something that already stares you in the face. Writing is, after all, just a craft.

But what I don't get is the insistence that the person behind these words, addressing me 'directly', knows me, knows my story, understands me deeply, and is willing to show compassion. Now that's a whole lot of knowledge in one basket. About an other you don't know.

The main question that begs itself here is this one:

What is it that marketers are missing when they act on assumption? When they know everything about the people they want to sell to?

How do they know what they know? Becasue of statistics? Demographics? Analytics of what works and what doesn't?

I'd say that what is missing is stamina and resilience. The very ingredients that give confidence.

Confidence is not your shining armor. It's your faith and trust in your dexterity, finger work coupled with robust demonstrations. Confidence is zero tricks.

Why am I suspicious of the way *The Copy Cure* sells? Let it be said that I don't doubt the value of a product I don't know, so I don't comment on the content that may very well be both valuable and well put together.

What I want to know is what makes seemingly competent people, who may have a good product in their hands, resort to tricks that are anything but robust.

§

As it happens, I never had big struggles. I was never in debt. I was never addicted, and I was never raised by mean chimpanzees who didn't share their bananas with me. I never had to overcome obstacles, find self-love, and live the life of my dreams.

There's a good, vivid image here that hooks. I can just picture the bananas that I didn't get to eat, even though that has never been my story.

I fail, however, to fall for debt and addiction because these are words that operate with an intangible sense of victimhood.

While some may find themselves nodding, 'yeah, man, I've been there, and it sucked,' I don't feel moved by this generality.

What I'm trying to say is that without doing the footwork, merely pressing on the button that we call 'share your vulnerable story' will only get you to where you bedazzle a whole lot of people with content devoid of content.

JUST THINK:

What good is a conman who sells you the world, but teaches you nothing about the world?

What good is a conman who enchants you, but has no solid skills for anything?

**Don't think** that just because a magician is in the picture, he is also able to magic your world in a way that's useful to you.

**Don't think** that just because something is popular, it's also the best. When the clarion's call heralds an opinion, this opinion is not fair judgment or discernment.

**Don't think** that just because many fall for it, the world that's offered also matches the world that's promised.

§

When the Magician works for me, in a world that's full of fanfare and wonder, he represents something that an athlete knows:

Focus and stamina.

Focus and stamina as a resilience pack is created in the mind. You can instruct the mind to be in the body, stay there and forget about its thoughts, positive or negative.

You can instruct the magician who wants to get there fast to remember to listen, focus and concentrate.

But where is this point of focus when you deal with the public, with people having different needs?

How can you listen to them all?

What world do you promise or herald for them all?

§

Russian scientists call this process of holistic awareness 'attention deconcentration', when your focus is on distributed attention, when your focus is on the margins of everything, including the center, but not on the center, not on the dot.

Free diver and water magician Natalia Molchanova, now vanished from this world while giving a private deep diving lesson, referred to her skills as being the skills of a warrior, a samurai, and one might add, a great Zen master.

A magician who is also a warrior, who is so good that he simply kills every trick he ever does, can create a world of magic out of empty consciousness, the consciousness that goes into a magic trick beyond the trick.

See, this is exactly what we find in the time it takes to go from 1 to 21: Empty consciousness.

Imagine approaching the public, the witnesses to your dexterous skills, from this emptiness, from a space that's completely free of judgment, personal involvement, and emotional distraction.

Can you focus on your world's edges and its guarded corners, and from this focus let your skills emerge as universal, yet addressing each and every one in the excited crowd you wish to touch with your enchantment?

Moreover, what is the premise for your touch?

People are waiting for this, for your resilient and robust skills, not for resounding blah blah.

You can be the secret agent bringing liberation to the ones ready for a new world.

If you can do that, enchant through skill and pedagogy, you will find that you don't need to use words or gestures as tools for expressing generalities.

You will use words and gestures to create pure worlds of magic, worlds that awaken your and others' awareness beyond anything you can even imagine.

§

REFERENCE:

For inspiration from the fascinating world of focus and attention, see *The Deepest Dive* by Alec Wilkinson, in *The New Yorker.* August 24, 2009.

# Give Yourself Time

Some would argue that the highest human art is knowing how to avoid transforming your anger into aggression.

Just imagine life not being about strategies of coping, but rather about avoiding events: avoiding an accident, if you're driving; avoiding twisting your ankle, if you're walking; avoiding running out of lamp oil, if you're seeking things in the dark; avoiding getting sunburnt, if you're out in the garden playing all day; avoiding domination, if you're trying to persuade others; avoiding indifference, if you're suspended; avoiding fear, if you're out camping in the wild.

Some would say, living a life of caution is a boring life. But what if caution is wise? What if caution is exciting because its highest expression is moderation and perfect balance?

Imagine being perfectly balanced and thus able to maintain perfect peace of mind.

I know that peace of mind seduces the hell out of me. Peace of mind exerts magnetic power over me. It makes me write tomes of poetry, all having titles that carry the word 'grace' in them.

Peace of mind 'thinks' nothing of struggle. It writes aggression off. If there's anger, it just flows. There's no coercion.

§

Much of the Buddhist teaching that fascinates me stresses the importance of knowing this, actually rather subtle, difference between anger and aggression.

Chögyam Trungpa Rimpoche built a whole empire by talking about this, about the art of rising to your angry self, and then giving it a lesson in radical acceptance. We are grateful to such masters.

Anger is good, aggression is bad.

We use 'good' and 'bad' here instrumentally, not because we believe in such division, but because it helps us understand what is at stake when dealing with beasts, with the ones who never seem to be on the same page as us.

First you fight with them, then you try to instruct them by the book in the high art of showing some discretion – no bullies, thank you – and then you go the diplomatic way, smoothing the relation.

Compromise is also a high art, but only if you can manage your resentment. Without such skill, you end up with a flow of hatred rather than a flow of peace.

When Force shows up, trying to overpower the problem in front of her, the Popesse following her keeps a record. In the process of describing the problem, you give yourself time to see if you get it right. How big is the problem exactly? What nature does it have?

Giving yourself time is also a high art. Giving yourself time to ask the question of what the purpose of anything is opens the gate to flow, to balance, to a perfect mix of the beast with the book.

JUST THINK:

When Force, the Popesse, and Temperance show up in this particular order, they invite you to consider these questions:

What are the strategies of coping with force? Anger operates with force, with physical and mental strength, and with impulsivity, the opposite of resilience. Impulsivity that lingers turns into stubbornness, and there's a short road from there to bullying.

Can you cultivate your anger? What book will be your good book? The one you go to every time you need to solve a conflict?

I go to popular sayings and proverbs. I find folk wisdom the best. New knowledge about anger management can be fascinating, and it can crack some skulls, but it never beats the common sense that folk wisdom has.

**Don't just assume** that the card of Strength is a representation of your power in unmediated form. No one can handle raw power.

**Don't just assume** that the card of the Popesse is your wisdom in unmediated form. No one is wise without experience.

**Don't just assume** that the card of Temperance is your healer in unmediated form. No one heals without first understanding the root of a problem.

§

My practice of contemplating with the Tarot cards, trumps and pip cards included, has always been a practice anchored in getting a sense of how things flow, or don't.

It takes time to figure out the power of flow. It takes time to figure out how you can transform what makes you tick like a bomb into listening to the pulse of your heart, and how it aligns with the pulse of the earth.

Perhaps this is the reason why influential occultists of the 19th century thought of the card of Temperance as a card of time, a card that blends our perception of past, present, and future, making temporality a matter of unity, not of distinct separations.

P.D. Ouspensky's book, *The Symbolism of the Tarot,* even insists that Temperance is time, not the Hermit, another favorite contender for time.

'The name of the angel is Time, he says, 'time in its most incomprehensible aspect.'

The premise for this observation is the fact that time doesn't flow in one direction only. It flows both ways, in and out of perspective.

§

If you can crack a problem by understanding its nature, you will see how flow makes everything transparent.

You will see the invisible, and understand the silent gaping of the mouth.

Your AH is waiting to be born, of ink and feather, words flowing from your pen, flying on your page, saying, 'give yourself time.'

Give yourself time, and you will understand the subtle burst of the mystery of the obvious.

§

## REFERENCES:

Although I read cards following the method of paying attention to the visual language of the cards at the formal level, which is to say that I look at color and design and then embodiment, function, gesture, and voice, I appreciate the poetic voice of the occultists when they describe the Tarot cards in terms of their participation in the transmission of mystery traditions.

Hence I recommend P.D. Ouspensky's *The Symbolism of the Tarot: Philosophy of Occultism in Pictures and Numbers.* Dover Publications, 1976.

For my own take, see my books, *Marseille Tarot: Towards the Art of Reading.* EyeCorner Press, 2014, and *The Oracle Travels Light: Principles of Magic with Cards.* EyeCorner Press, 2015.

For common sense wisdom, see Chögyam Tungpa Rimpoche's *Shambala: The Scared Path of the Warrior.* Shambala Publications, 1984.

∞

# Beyond Cards and Magic

These reflections here are part of the series of recorded lectures followed by a live Q&A session, BEYOND CARDS AND MAGIC.

## The Power of the Trumps: A Subtle Burst

is also available as a pack of eight video lectures, a recording of the live Q&A session that took place after the release of the lectures, and a pdf version of this book.

Visit
**cameliaelias.com**

§

BEYOND CARDS AND MAGIC
is about reading quirky, complex, tried and tested texts and grimoires, and whole cartomantic systems through the lens of the Tarot cards.

BEYOND CARDS AND MAGIC
opens a gate to the possibility to read with the cards against the grain, bust a few towers, and laugh.

Lightning Source UK Ltd.
Milton Keynes UK
UKOW07f1301090417
298701UK00007B/12/P